21 Days of

Fasting and Prayer

The Point of the Prayer is the
Prayer Point!

SARAH MORGAN

Copyright © 2016 SARAH MORGAN

ISBN: 978-0-9859690-7-3

MORGAN PUBLISHING

21 Days of Fasting and Prayer: The Point of Prayer is the Prayer Point!

Published by Morgan Publishing
3701 Inglewood, CA 90278
Redondo Beach, CA 90047
888-320-5622

JOIN THE MOVEMENT! CONNECT WITH US ON:
www.prayeracademy.org
www.instagram.com/prayeracademyglobal
www.facebook.com/prayeracademyglobal
www.twitter.com/prayeracademy_

ISBN 978-0-9859690-7-3

Cover Design by Dee Shervell
Editing and typesetting by www.freshreign.com

Dedication

This is dedicated to all praying warriors, intercessors, travailing women and wayfaring men in Gods Army. Your seasons of fasting and prayer have changed the course of your generation more than you will ever know. I pray that generations yet unborn will encounter GOD because of your sacrifice.

"God is not unjust, He will not forget your work and labor of love, which ye have shewed toward His name, in that ye have ministered to the saints, and do minister" (Hebrews 6:1).

Yours truly,

Sarah Morgan

Table of Contents

Preface

These Prayer Point books came out of a season of consecration through fasting and prayer, which was annually observed by *Prayer Academy* Students across the country to end the year strong.

At the end of last year in October, I was led by the Holy Spirit to extend this invitation to the nation, via the medium of Periscope where intercessors and prayer warriors joined me to pray daily on our beloved broadcast Prayer Altar Scope where to grow by the Grace of God.

Since that first cooperate fast, the *Prayer Altar Scope* family has observed several fasts together praying for families, relationships, marriages, churches, communities, cities, regions, our nation and the world standing on 2 Chronicles 7:14-15,

" If My people, who are called by My name, shall humble themselves, pray, seek, crave, and require of necessity My face and turn from their wicked ways, then will I hear from heaven, forgive their sin, and heal their land. **Now My eyes will be open and My ears attentive to prayer offered in this place."**

What place was God speaking about? *The Place of Prayer is the Place of Power.*

In order for everyone to pray the same thing from their respective regions, cities and States, through the medium of technology and social media e.g. Facebook: @prayeracademyglobal, website: www.womenofvisionla.org, and Twitter: @prayeracademy_; we loaded the Prayer Points daily with the help of Prophetess Karla Allen, also known as, Coach K~. [Shout out to Coach K~]. Consequently, as we gathered daily at the Prayer Altar, the seekers requested that we put the Prayer Points in print for future seasons of Prayer and Fasting, individually and corporately, hence now our newest addition to our Prayer Arsenal, *The Point of Prayer is The Prayer Point* series:

1. 7 Days of Fasting and Prayer
2. 21 Days of Fasting and Prayer
3. 30 Days of Fasting and Prayer

Remember, "Anything that is not birthed out of Prayer is Illegal."

Yours Truly,

Sarah Morgan

Introduction

Fight the good fight of faith . . . (1 Timothy 6:12).

Throughout history, God has called on His people to humble themselves through fasting and prayer. Fasting is a spiritual weapon God uses to advance His kingdom, change the destiny of nations, spark revival, and bring victory in people's lives. There is something powerful that happens when we voluntarily humble ourselves, seek God's will, and agree with Him for His purposes to be fulfilled.

As a spiritual family of Praying Warriors and Watchmen on the Walls, we purpose to begin and end each Year with a season of prayer and fasting. It is our way of humbling ourselves before God and consecrating to Him the upcoming New Year and thanking Him for crowning the year with goodness. It is also the time when we corporately come into agreement and believe together for breakthroughs in our personal lives, our families, our finances, and our churches.

One of the highlights is always seeing and hearing testimonies of how God answers over and beyond what people ask. Over the years, as a result of this time of fasting and prayer, I have seen people receive healing, salvation, promotion, direction, family restoration, miraculous provision, and tremendous growth in their fellowships and churches.

As you begin your fast, believe in your heart, by faith, that this is your year of miracles and answered prayers.

Declare a holy fast; call a sacred assembly. Summon the elders and all who live in the land to the house of the LORD your God, and cry out to the LORD (Joel 1:14).

. . . "Consecrate yourselves, for tomorrow the LORD will do amazing things among you" (Joshua 3:5).

Believe God for victories and breakthroughs in every area of your life as you begin and end the year strong in Jesus' name. When a man is willing to set aside the legitimate appetites of the body to concentrate on the work of praying, he is demonstrating that he means business, and that he is seeking God with all his heart, and will not let God go unless He answers.

Practical Prayer and Fasting Guide

WHY Should You Fast?

1. Jesus fasted.

"Then Jesus was led by the Spirit into the desert to be tempted by the devil. After fasting forty days and forty nights, he was hungry" (Matthew 4:1-2).

"Jesus returned to Galilee in the power of the Spirit, and news about him spread through the whole countryside" (Luke 4:14).

Before He began His ministry, Jesus fasted forty days and ate nothing. He knew He was going to need spiritual strength and stamina to fulfill His purposes. Fasting makes us physically weak, but spiritually strong and prepares us to do God's work.

2. Fasting is an act of humility and consecration.

...I put on sackcloth and humbled myself with fasting... (Psalm 35:13).

Humility results in the grace of God. When we humble ourselves in prayer, we have instant access to the heart of God. As we deny ourselves as an act of consecration, we are better able to exercise self-control and keep our emotions and desires under control.

3. Fasting helps us become sensitive to the Holy Spirit.

While they were worshiping the Lord and fasting, the Holy Spirit said, "Set apart for me Barnabas and Saul for the work to which I have called them" (Acts 13:2).

When we deny ourselves of our natural cravings, our spiritual antennas become sharper. We become more sensitive to the voice of the Holy Spirit as we divest ourselves of worldly distractions. We are better able to focus on God and submit to His will. This opens the door for the Holy Spirit into our lives.

Fasting brings revival.

> . . . *in the first year of his reign, I, Daniel, understood from the Scriptures, according to the word of the LORD given to Jeremiah the prophet, that the desolation of Jerusalem would last seventy years. So I turned to the Lord God and pleaded with him in prayer and petition, in fasting, and in sackcloth and ashes* (Daniel 9:2-3).

Fasting helps us prevail in prayer and intercession. Daniel understood that Israel was headed for destruction. He also knew that in times like these, there is only one recourse— intercession through praying and fasting. Throughout human history, God has brought revival and delivered nations from destruction in response to prayer and fasting.

4. Fasting is healthy.

Fasting cleanses your digestive system from toxins. Doctors consider fasting a cure for certain allergies and diseases. By learning to deny ourselves and exercising discipline, fasting breaks unhealthy addictions in our lives.

BEFORE you Fast...

1. Be in faith!

Prayerfully and thoughtfully ask the Holy Spirit for guidance. Be clear and specific about your faith goals in your personal life, family, finances, and church. These are what you will believe God for during the fast and the entire year to come.

Expect God to answer. Maintain a thankful heart throughout and after the fast.

2. Commit to a type of fast.

We encourage everyone to commit to a "water only" or "liquid fast" during this season of prayer and fasting. However, we understand some are unable to do so because of certain circumstances such as pregnancy, a physically demanding profession, or medical conditions. If you belong to this category, there are alternatives—you may choose to do a combination fast.

You may do a liquid fast for three days and then one meal a day fast for the next four, for example, or any other combination according to your need or situation. Pray about the kind of fast you will undertake and commit to it. Do not decide on a day-to-day basis. Commit before the fast, be determined, and ask God for grace.

3. Plan your calendar.
Limit your physical and social activities during this period. You need to conserve physical energy and devote more time to prayer and reading the Bible.

4. Prepare spiritually.

More than anything, this fast is a time when we believe God for a fresh encounter with Him. Be prepared to have the Holy Spirit put His finger on an area in your life that needs transformation. Repentance is the foundation of prayer and fasting. Be ready to repent, change, and be transformed. Surrender everything to Him, and be completely open.

5. Prepare physically.

Be smart as you enter into this fast. Avoid food that is high in sugar and fat. Prior to the fast, try and eat raw fruit and vegetables only. Consult a physician if necessary.

> *"Go, gather together all the Jews who are in Susa, and fast for me. Do not eat or drink for three days, night or day. I and my maids will fast as you do. When this is done, I will go to the king, even though it is against the law. And if I perish, I perish"* (Esther 4:16).

Finally, fasting reduces the power of self so that the Holy Spirit can do a more intense work within us.

PREPARING to Fast:

1. **Seek the Lord.**

    a. Commit to prayer and Bible reading during the times you usually allocate for meals. The tithes belong to the Lord. Therefore, endeavor to give a tenth of your day [twenty-four hours] which is 2 hours and forty minutes during your consecration, and you will reap the abundant benefits.

    b. Join at least one prayer meeting in your local church, prayer group or prayer partners. Cooperate prayer is powerful, one can put a thousand to flight and two ten thousand (Due. 32:30).

    c. Try and connect with daily prayer meetings scheduled in every local area whether by phone, periscope, etc. throughout the fast.

Commit to change

d. Whatever God tells you or puts His finger upon, apply it immediately. If you need to make restitution, directly contact people with whom you have broken relationships. If there are habits that need to change, make the adjustment immediately. Ask your group leader to hold you accountable.

BE Practical

e. Avoid medical and even natural herbal drugs. However, if you are under medication, these should only be withdrawn upon the advice of your doctor.

f. Limit your physical activity and exercise. If you have a workout routine, adjust it accordingly. A daily two to five-kilometer walk should be your maximum amount of exercise during an extended fast.

g. Rest as much as you can.

h. Maintain an attitude of prayer throughout the day. Intercede for your family, pastors, church, nation, our missionaries, world missions, etc.

i. Drink plenty of clean water.

j. As your body adjusts, be prepared for temporary bouts of physical weakness as well as mental annoyances like impatience, irritability, and anxiety (withdraw from the withdrawal symptoms).

k. Reintroduce solid food gradually.

l. *"When you fast, do not look somber as the hypocrites do, for they disfigure their faces to show men they are fasting. I tell you the truth; they have received their reward in full. But when you fast, put oil on your head and wash your face, so that it will not be obvious to men that you are fasting, but only to your Father, who is unseen; and your Father, who sees what is done in secret, will reward you"* (Matthew 6:16-18).

"The record of the whole Bible indicates that prayer and fasting combined; constitute the strongest weapon committed to God's believers." Dr. Mary Ruth Swop

Continue praying

m. Don't let your prayer life end on the day you finish the fast. Build from the momentum you gained during the fast. Let it transform your prayer and devotional life. Carry the newfound passion with you into the every New Season.

Be expectant

n. Be in faith and believe God to answer your prayers soon! Don't give up; persevere in prayer even if you don't see the answers immediately. Make sure you keep the copy of your prayer points. You can check it at the end of the year and see how God has answered your prayers. It can be your thanksgiving list at the end of the year.

"Paul and Barnabas appointed elders for them in each church and, with prayer and fasting, committed them to the Lord, in whom they had put their trust" (Acts 14:23).

o. Our prayer and fasting give us the opportunity to realign our lives according to His will and consecrate the coming year to Him. As we humble ourselves corporately to Him in prayer, we can expect Him to move mightily in our midst. God's will is for all of us to experience breakthrough and victory in our lives.

p. Be in faith for God to move miraculously in your life this year beyond what you can ask or imagine. You have a fresh mandate. Be ready to accomplish greater things for God next year and the years to come!

*Now to him who is able to do immeasurably more than all we ask or imagine, according to his power that is at work within us . . . (*Ephesians 3:20).

"Draw nigh to God, and he will draw nigh to you. Cleanse your hands, ye sinners; and purify your hearts, ye double minded. Be afflicted, and mourn, and weep: let your laughter be turned to mourning, and your joy to heaviness. Humble yourselves in the sight of the Lord, and he shall lift you up" (James 4:8-10).

Journal

Based on John 1:17, where does truth come from?

_____

_____

What did Jesus say we must do so that we can know the truth (John 8:31, 32)? What is the result of knowing the truth? Respond and reflect

_____

_____

_____

_____

Ask God to reveal some lies of the enemy you may have believed that need to be replaced with the truth.

_____

_____

_____

_____

Spend some time searching the Scriptures and praying, then write down what you hear the Holy Spirit saying to you.

_____

_____

_____

ARE YOU READY to begin your 21-day pursuit?

We give ourselves to prayer and fasting as a corporate body, but more so as Watchmen on the wall! For three weeks of the month of your choice dedicate to God, soul, mind, body and spirit. YOU WILL DEAL WITH YOUR SPIRITUAL HUNGER FIRST! Jesus promises in Matthew 5:6, *"Blessed are they which do hunger and thirst after righteousness; for they shall be filled."*

The combination of fasting and praying is not a fad or a novelty approach to spiritual discipline. Fasting and praying are not part of a human-engineered method or plan. Fasting and Praying is not the means to manipulate a situation or to create a circumstance. Fasting and praying is a Bible-based discipline that is appropriate for all believers. Fasting and praying breaks the yoke of bondage and brings about a release of God's presence, power, and provision.

Biblical fasting is going without food,[Abstinence]. The noun translated "fast" or "a fasting" is *tsom* in the Hebrew and *nesteia* in the Greek language. It means the voluntary abstinence from food. The literal Hebrew translation would be *"not to eat."* The literal Greek means to abstain or *"no food."*

You may decide to go without entertainment and social media outlets. You may put down your television remote or newspaper or perhaps some hobby or form of recreation. I encourage you to add this form of discipline to your fasting, as long as you specifically replace it with prayer. However, to be biblically accurate, fasting has to do with our abstaining from food.

DON'T JUST GIVE IT UP! REPLACE IT! Just to "give up" something is a frivolous approach to fasting. We must replace what we fast from with prayer! Spiritual fasting involves our hearts and the way in which we relate to and trust God.

Fasting gives us discernment and strength to follow

through on what God will reveal to us about circumstances in our lives, a direction we are to take, or a command we are to follow. To control one's eating is a valid reason to fast—just not the main reason. The purpose is not the number of pounds you might lose during a fast, but rather, trusting God to help you regain mastery over food during a fast. Jesus said, *"...The spirit indeed is willing, but the flesh is weak" (Matt. 26:41).*

Fasting is a means of bringing the flesh into submission to the Lord so He can strengthen us in our mastery over our own selves. Fasting in the flesh makes us stronger to stand against the temptations of the flesh. God promises to help us as we overcome the flesh and put all carnal temptations into subjection.

Use this devotion guide as a focus for your prayer points. This will allow you to center in prayer and receive the Promise of agreement.

In conjunction with the daily prayer points, read the Gospel of Saint John, one chapter a day for the 21 days. Prayerfully meditate on the Word, and the Spirit of God will minister deeply the heart of the Father and Son. *"Again I say unto you, that if two of you shall agree on earth as touching anything that they shall ask, it shall be done for them of my Father, which is in heaven" (*Matthew" 18:19). May His Grace abound to you as His **Sufficiency** becomes your **Efficiency** in Jesus' name.

ALWAYS REMEMBER TO
- Pray for our Leaders, Political and Ecclesiastical.
- Pray for our Nation and Families.
- Pray for the Economy and that Violence and Bloodshed Will no longer be heard in our streets.
- Pray for the Peace of Jerusalem.

*"May the Lord bless thee and keep thee; may he cause his face to shine upon thee. May he be gracious unto thee and your house, and grant thee peace; shalom" (*Numbers 6:24-26).

Privileged to serve and committed to pray, *Sarah Morgan*

Day 1

Key Verse: Matthew 6:33

"But seek ye first the kingdom of God, and his righteousness; and all these things shall be added unto you".

Prayer Points: Teach me to seek you first in all things.

Definitions:

Seek

- To try and locate or discover.
- To search for.
- To endeavor to obtain or to reach.
- To go to or toward.
- To inquire for.
- To request.
- To make a search.

Seek and you shall find.

Deuteronomy 4:29, *"But if from thence thou shalt seek the Lord thy God,* ***thou shalt find him,*** *if thou seek him* ***with all thy heart and with all thy soul."***

> ➤ Father God, as I seek for you with all my heart and soul, which is my mind, my will, my emotions and being, let me find you, in Jesus' name.

2 Chronicles 7:14, *"If my people, which are called by my name, shall humble themselves, and pray, and seek my face, and turn from their wicked ways; then* *will **I hear from heaven, and will forgive their sin, and will heal their land**."*.

> ➤ Father God, as one of Your people, called by Your name, I humble myself through fasting and prayer. I seek Your Face and not Your hand. I repent by changing my mind and completely turning from the wicked ways of my heart, thoughts, words and deeds. Incline your ear to hear, forgive me of all my sins and heal every area of our land, in Jesus' name.

Ezra 7:10, *"For Ezra had prepared his heart to seek the **law of the Lord, and to do it, and to teach** in Israel statutes and judgments."*

> ➤ Father God, as I've prepared my heart to seek Your Law which is Your Word, give me the grace to be a doer of your Word and likewise teach others in Jesus' name.

Ezra 8:21, *"Then I proclaimed a fast there, at the river of Ahava, that we might afflict ourselves before our God, **to seek of him a right way for us**, and for our little ones, and for all our substance."*

> ➤ Father God, as I fast and pray show me the right way to live, the right way to talk, love, and the way to represent you to my little ones and the world in Jesus' name.

Psalm 9:10, *"And they that know thy name will put their trust in thee: for thou, Lord, **hast not forsaken them that seek thee**."*

Psalm 34:10, *"The young lions do lack, and suffer hunger: **but they that seek the Lord shall not want any good thing**."*

Psalm 40:16, *"Let all those **that seek thee rejoice and be glad***

in thee: *let such as love thy salvation say continually, The Lord."*

Psalm 119:45, *"And I will walk at liberty: for I seek thy precepts."*

Proverbs 8:17, *"I love them that love me; and those that seek me early shall find me."*

Day 2

Key Verses: Psalm 51:1-13

Psalm, 51;1-13, *"Have mercy upon me, O God, according to thy lovingkindness: according unto the multitude of thy tender mercies blot out my transgressions. 2 Wash me thoroughly from mine iniquity, and cleanse me from my sin. 3 For I acknowledge my transgressions: and my sin is ever before me. 4 Against thee, thee only, have I sinned, and done this evil in thy sight: that thou mightest be justified when thou speakest, and be clear when thou judgest. 5 Behold, I was shapen in iniquity; and in sin did my mother conceive me. 6 Behold, thou desirest truth in the inward parts: and in the hidden part thou shalt make me to know wisdom. 7 Purge me with hyssop, and I shall be clean: wash me, and I shall be whiter than snow. 8 Make me to hear joy and gladness; that the bones which thou hast broken may rejoice. 9 Hide thy face from my sins, and blot out all mine iniquities. 10 Create in me a clean heart, O God; and renew a right spirit within me. 11 Cast me not away from thy presence; and take not thy holy spirit from me. 12 Restore unto me the joy of thy salvation; and uphold me with thy free spirit. 13 Then will I teach transgressors thy ways; and sinners shall be converted unto thee.*

Prayer Point: Purify my heart and motives.

Definitions:

Purify
- To rid of impurities.
- To get rid of foreign or objectionable elements.
- To free from moral or spiritual defilement.

- To free a person from sin or guilt, and to make one clean

Motive
- The reason for a certain course of action
- The inducement and incentive that prompts an action, whether conscious or unconscious

Proverbs 16:2 [AMP], *"The plans and reflections of the heart belong to man, but the [wise] answer of the tongue is from the Lord. All the ways of a man are clean and innocent in his own eyes [and he may see nothing wrong with his actions],* **But the Lord weighs and examines the motives and intents [of the heart and knows the truth].** *Commit your works to the Lord [submit and entrust them to Him], and your plans will succeed [if you respond to His will and guidance].*

Jeremiah 17:9 *"The heart is deceitful above all things and it is extremely sick;* **who can understand it fully and know its secret motives?***"*

2 Corinthians 5:10, *"For we [believers will be called to account and] must all appear before the judgment seat of Christ, so that each one may be repaid for what has been done in the body, whether good or bad* **[that is, each will be held responsible for his actions, purposes, goals, motives**—*the use or misuse of his time, opportunities and abilities]."*

Philippians 2:3, *"Do nothing from selfishness or empty conceit* **[through factional motives, or strife]**, *but with [an attitude of] humility [being neither arrogant nor self- righteous], regard others as more important than yourselves."*

James 4:3, *"You ask [God for something] and do not receive it,* **because you ask [a] with wrong motives [out of selfishness or with an unrighteous agenda]**, *so that [when you get what you want] you may spend it on your[hedonistic] desires."*

Malachi 3:3, *"And He shall sit as a refiner and purifier of silver:* **and he shall purify the sons of Levi, and purge them as gold and silver,** *that they may offer unto the Lord an offering in righteousness."*

➤ Father God, I give You permission to sit as a Refiner and Purifier of silver and cleanse and purify my heart of all impurities and defilements in Jesus' name.

Day 3

Key Verses: Psalm 101

I will sing of mercy and judgment: unto thee, O Lord, will I sing. 2 I will behave myself wisely in a perfect way. O when wilt thou come unto me? I will walk within my house with a perfect heart. 3 I will set no wicked thing before mine eyes: I hate the work of them that turn aside; it shall not cleave to me. 4 A froward heart shall depart from me: I will not know a wicked person. 5 Whoso privily slandereth his neighbor, him will I cut off: him that hath an high look and a proud heart will not I suffer. 6 Mine eyes shall be upon the faithful of the land, that they may dwell with me: he that walketh in a perfect way, he shall serve me. 7 He that worketh deceit shall not dwell within my house: he that telleth lies shall not tarry in my sight. 8 I will early destroy all the wicked of the land; that I may cut off all wicked doers from the city of the Lord.

Prayer Point: Shield my eyes/ears from unrighteousness and cause me to behave wisely.

Definition:

Shield
- a person or thing that provides protection.

*unto Abram in a vision, saying, Fear not, Abram: **I am thy shield,** and thy exceeding great reward."*

2 Samuel 22:3, *"The God of my rock; in him will I trust: **He is my shield,** and the horn of my salvation, my high tower, and my refuge, my savior; thou savest me from violence."*

2 Samuel 22:36, *"Thou hast also given me **the shield of thy salvation:** and thy gentleness hath made me great."*

Psalm 3:3, *"But thou, O Lord, art a shield for me; my glory, and the lifter up of mine head."*

Psalm 28:7, *"The Lord is **my strength and my shield;** my heart trusted in him, and I am helped: therefore my heart greatly rejoiceth; and with my song will I praise him."*

Psalm 33:20, *"Our soul waiteth for the Lord: **He is our help and our shield."***

> ➢ Father God, Shield my eyes and ears from righteousness and cause me to behave wisely, in Jesus' name.

Day 4

Key Verses: James 3:1-12

James 3:1-12, *"7 "For every kind of beasts, and of birds, and of serpents, and of things in the sea, is tamed, and hath been tamed of mankind: 8 But the tongue can no man tame; it is an unruly evil, full of deadly poison."*

Prayer Point: Tame my tongue and train it to speak life.

Definition:

Tame

> ➤ To change from an uncontrolled or disorderly to a controlled state

Job 6:24, *"Teach me, and I will hold my tongue: and cause me to understand wherein I have erred."*

Job 27:4, *"My lips shall not speak wickedness, nor my tongue utter deceit."*

Psalm 39:1, *"I said, I will take heed to my ways, that I sin not with my tongue: I will keep my mouth with a bridle, while the wicked is before me."*

Psalm 71:24, *"My tongue also shall talk of thy righteousness all the day long: for they are confounded, for they are brought unto shame that seek my hurt."*

> ➤ Father God, let your Word tame my tongue that it extol your goodness, in Jesus' name.

Day 5

Key Verses: Romans 12:1-2

Romans 12:*2* *"And be not conformed to this world: but be ye transformed by the renewing of your mind, that ye may prove what is that good, and acceptable, and perfect, will of God."*

Prayer Point: Transform my mind and thoughts.

Definitions:

Transform
- ➢ To change the appearance and form markedly.
- ➢ To change the nature, function, or condition of; convert.
- ➢ Radically altered radically in form and function.

Renew
- • To make new or as in new again; restore.

Isaiah 40:31, *" But they that wait upon the Lord shall **renew their strength,** they shall mount up with wings as eagles; and not faint."*

Psalm 51:10, *"Create in me a clean heart, O God; and renew a right spirit within me."*

Psalm 103:5, *"Who satisfieth thy mouth with good things; so that thy youth is renewed like the eagles."*

2 Corinthians 4:16, *"For which cause we faint not; but though our outward man perish, yet the inward man is renewed day by day."*

Ephesians 4:23, *"And be renewed in the spirit of your mind;"*

> ➤ Father God, let me not be conformed to ways of this world, but let me be transformed and renewed daily in Jesus' name.

Day 6

Key Verses: 1 Corinthians 13:1-7

1 Corinthians 13:1-4 (MSG), *"[The Way of Love] If I speak with human eloquence and angelic ecstasy **but don't love**, I'm nothing but the creaking of a rusty gate. If I speak God's Word with power, revealing all his mysteries and making everything plain as day, and if I have faith that says to a mountain, "Jump," and it jumps, **but I don't love**, I'm nothing. If I give everything I own to the poor and even go to the stake to be burned as a martyr, **but I don't love**, I've gotten nowhere. So, no matter what I say, what I believe, and what I do, **I'm bankrupt without love.***

Prayer Point: Teach me how to love like you.

God is love. Love is the fundamental essence of His nature and character—His very being. God is perfect in love. God's love is manifested by His absolutely pure desire to care for, share and give.

In our day, most define love as some type of feeling. We "fall in love," or two people meet and it is "love at first sight." But the world's love is a selfish matter. If you are attractive to me, be nice to me, meet my needs and love me I in return will "love" you.

The world's love is based on getting something from someone else. The world does not give love when there is no personal benefit. If you do not please me, then I have no love for you. Thus, for the world love must be earned by making someone else feel good.

Powerful emotions may accompany love, but it is the commitment of the will that holds true biblical love steadfast and unchanging. Emotions may change, but a commitment to love, biblically, endures and is the hallmark of a disciple of Christ. Emotions will vary, but a commitment which has its basis in biblical love will not be affected by overwhelming emotions of one's circumstances. Our example of true love is shown in God's love for the sinner. Romans 5:8 says *". . .commendeth his love toward us, in that, while we were yet sinners, Christ died for us. "* The lost sinner living in rebellion and sin is still loved by the Lord. He loved us enough to die for us and pay our sin debt while we were sinning against Him. This shows that true biblical love is a matter of will, not of emotion. God chose to love us, and His love was not based on our merit.

Day 7

Key Verse: 1 Timothy 1:2

1 Timothy 1:2, *"Unto Timothy, my own son in the faith: Grace, mercy, and peace, from God our Father and Jesus Christ our Lord."*

Prayer Point: Grant me Grace, mercy and peace for things beyond my control.

Definitions:
Grace

- Unmerited, unearned, undeserved favor of God.
- Divine enablement and empowerment.
- God giving us something we do not deserve.

Mercy

- God not giving us what we deserve as in verdict.
- God's Veto PEN.

Ruth 2:13, *"She said, "Oh sir, **such grace, such kindness—I don't deserve it.** You've touched my heart, treated me like one of your own. And I don't even belong here!"*

> ➤ Father God, let people I know not show me undeserved Grace, mercy and peace, in Jesus' name.

Job 29:1-6, *"[When God Was Still by My Side] Job now resumed his response: "Oh, how I long for the good old days, when God took such very good care of me. He always held a lamp before me and I walked through the dark by its light. Oh, how I miss those golden year when **God's friendship graced my home,** When the Mighty One was still by my side and my children were all around me, when everything was going my way, and nothing seemed too difficult."*

32

> ➢ Father God, may your **friendship Grace, Favor and Empower** my home and family, in Jesus' name.

> ➢ May my children be around me and may all my difficulties disappear, in Jesus' name.

Psalm 10:15-16, *"Break the wicked right arm, break all the evil left arms. Search and destroy every sign of crime.* ***God's grace and order win****; godlessness loses."*

> ➢ Father God, let Your Grace and order win over all evil and wickedness, in Jesus' name.

Psalm 145:8, *"God is all mercy and* ***grace****— not quick to anger, is rich in love."*

Acts 14:23-26, *"Paul and Barnabas handpicked leaders in each church. After praying—their prayers intensified by fasting—they presented these new leaders to the Master to whom they had entrusted their lives. Working their way back through Pisidia, they came to Pamphylia and preached in Perga. Finally, they made it to Attalia and caught a ship back to Antioch, where it had all started—****launched by God's grace and now safely home by God's grace."***

> ➢ Father God, let Your Grace launch me into my next season, place and dimension, in Jesus' name.

Psalm 51:1-3, *"[A David Psalm, After He Was Confronted by Nathan About the Affair with Bathsheba]* Generous in love— God, give grace! **Huge in mercy—wipe out my bad record.** Scrub away my guilt, soak out my sins in your laundry. I know how bad I've been; my sins are staring me down."

> ➢ Father God, in the **abundance and hugeness of your mercy,** wipe out my bad record, scrub away my guilt and soak out my sins in Your Divine Laundry, in Jesus' name.

Key Verses: Psalm 37:7

Psalm 37:7 (KJV), "*7 Rest in the Lord, and wait **patiently** for him: fret not thyself because of him who prospereth in his way, because of the man who bringeth wicked devices to pass.*"

Prayer Point: Help me be patient when I'm ready for change.

Definitions:
Patient

- Patient means to be able to accept or tolerate delays, problems, or suffering without becoming annoyed or anxious.
- Patient means forbearing, uncomplaining, tolerant and resigned.

Psalm 40:1, *"I waited patiently for the Lord; and he inclined unto me, and heard my cry."*

➤ Father God, teach me how to wait patiently for You, and hear my cry, in Jesus' name.

Ecclesiastes 7:8, *"Better is the end of a thing than the beginning thereof: and **the patient in spirit** is better than the proud in spirit."*

➤ Father God, teach my spirit to be **patient** and not proud, in Jesus' name.

➤ Let the end of every bad situation in my, be better than how it began, in Jesus' name.

Romans 2:7, *"To them who by **patient** continuance in well doing seek for glory and honor and immortality, eternal life."*
"

Romans 12:12, *"Rejoicing in hope; **patient in tribulation;** continuing instant in prayer."*

➤ Father God, teach me how to be **patient** in tribulation, and steadfast in prayer, in Jesus' name.

Day 9

Key Verses: 2 Peter 1:7

2 Peter 1:7, *"And to godliness brotherly* **kindness** *and to brotherly* **kindness** *charity."*

Prayer Point: Cause me to be kind whether others deserve it or not.

Definitions:
Kind:
- Gracious and kindhearted.
- Kindly imply a sympathetic attitude toward others.
- A willingness to do good or give pleasure.
- Kind is to be affectionate, amiable charitable.
- Compassionate, considerate, cordial, courteous.
- Thoughtful, tolerant, and benevolent.

Ephesians 4:32, *"And be ye* **kind** *one to another, tenderhearted, forgiving one another, even as God for Christ's sake hath forgiven you.:"*

> ➤ Father God, help me and teach me to be kind and tenderhearted, forgiving all for Christ's sake, in Jesus' name.

Luke 6:35, *"But love ye your enemies, and do good, and lend, hoping for nothing again; and your reward shall be great, and ye shall be the children of the Highest: for he is* **kind** *unto the unthankful and to the evil."*

- Father God, teach me to love my enemies, do good and be kind to the unthankful and to the evil doers, in Jesus' name.

Day 10

Key Verses: Psalm 37:27, Philippians 1:6

Psalm 37:27, *"Depart from evil, and do good and dwell for evermore."*

Philippians 1:6, *"Being confident of this very thing, that he which hath begun a **good** work in you will perform it until the day of Jesus Christ:"*

Prayer Point: Remind me to be **good** to others.

Definitions:

Good

- Being positive or desirable in nature.
- Having the qualities that are desirable or.
- Distinguishing in a particular thing.
- Of moral excellence; upright: *a good person.*
- Benevolent; kind: *a good soul; a good heart.*
- Well-behaved.
- Socially correct
- Worthy of respect; honorable

Psalm 37:27, *"Depart from evil, and do **good** and dwell for evermore."*

Psalm 38:20, *"They also that render evil for **good** are mine adversaries; because I follow the thing that **good** is."*

Ephesians 6:7, *"With **good** will doing service, as to the Lord, and not to men."*

Ephesians 6:8, *"Knowing that whatsoever **good** thing any man doeth, the same shall he receive of the Lord, whether he be bond or free."*

Philippians 4:8, *"Finally, brethren, whatsoever things are true, whatsoever things are honest, whatsoever things are just, whatsoever things are pure, whatsoever things are lovely, whatsoever things are of **good** report; if there be any virtue, and if there be any praise, think on these things."*

- Father God, help me and teach me how good and be good to all, in Jesus' name.

Day 11

Key Verses: 1 Corinthians 6:18-20

1 Corinthians 6:18-20 (KJV), *"18 Flee **fornication**. Every sin that a man doeth is without the body; but he that committeth **fornication** sinneth against his own body. 19 What? know ye not that your body is the temple of the Holy Ghost which is in you, which ye have of God, and ye are not your own? 20 For ye are bought with a price: **therefore glorify God in your body, and in your spirit, which are God's.**"*

Prayer Point: Show me how to be faithful to my spouse or keep me pure and celibate while I wait on a spouse.

Definitions:

Fornication

- Voluntary sexual intercourse between two unmarried persons or two persons not married to each other.

Adultery

- Voluntary sexual intercourse between a married person and someone other than his or her lawful spouse.

Matthew 19:9, *"And I say unto you, whosoever shall put away his wife, except it be for fornication, and shall marry another, committeth adultery: and whoso marrieth her which is put away doth commit adultery."*

1 Corinthians 6:18, *"Flee fornication. Every sin that a man doeth is without the body; but he that committeth fornication sinneth against his own body."*

1 Corinthians 7:2, *"Nevertheless, to avoid* **fornication**, *let every man have his own wife, and let every woman have her own husband."*

1 Corinthians 10:8, *"Neither let us commit* **fornication**, *as some of them committed, and fell in one day three and twenty thousand."*

Ephesians 5:3, *"But* **fornication**, *and all uncleanness, or covetousness, let it not be once named among you, as becometh saints;"*

Colossians 3:5, *"Mortify therefore your members which are upon the earth;* **fornication**, *uncleanness, inordinate affection, evil concupiscence, and covetousness, which is idolatry:"*

1 Thessalonians 4:3, *For this is the will of God, even your sanctification, that ye should abstain from* **fornication**:

> ➢ Father God, give me the grace to flee from fornication and abstain from the sin of adultery, in Jesus' name.

Day 12

Key Verses: Ephesians 6:4, Colossians 3:21, Deuteronomy 6:6-9

> **Deuteronomy 6:6-9** (KJV), "*6 And these words, which I command thee this day, shall be in thine heart: 7 And thou shalt teach them diligently unto thy children, and shalt talk of them when thou sittest in thine house, and when thou walkest by the way, and when thou liest down, and when thou risest up. 8 And thou shalt bind them for a sign upon thine hand, and they shall be as frontlets between thine eyes. 9 And thou shalt write them upon the posts of thy house, and on thy gates.*"

Ephesians 6:4 King (KJV*), "4 And, ye fathers provoke not your children to wrath: but bring them up in the nurture and admonition of the Lord.*"

Colossians 3:21 (KJV*), "21 Fathers, provoke not your children to anger, lest they be discouraged.*"

Prayer Point: Teach me how to be gentle toward the children I have authority and influence over.

Definitions:
Provoke

- To incite to anger or resentment.
- To stir to action or feeling: *a remark that provoked me to act.*
- To give rise to; bring about something *that provoked uproar.*
- To bring about deliberately; induce: *provoke a fight.* These verbs mean to move a person to action or

feeling or to summon something into being by so moving a person.

Provoke

- often merely states the consequences produced:

  ➤ Father God, teach me how not to provoke my children or any other person to act or react inappropriately, in Jesus' name.

Day 13

Key Verses: 1 Peter 1:5-8

1 Peter 1:5-8, *"And besides this, giving all diligence, add to your faith virtue; and to virtue knowledge; And to knowledge temperance; and to temperance patience; and to patience godliness; And to godliness brotherly kindness; and to brotherly kindness charity. For if these things be in you, and abound, they make you that ye shall be barren nor unfruitful in the knowledge of our Lord Jesus Christ."*

Prayer Point: Help me to uphold self-control in my mouth, body, and   finances.

Definitions:
Self-control
- the ability to control one's **emotions**, **behavior**, and desires to obtain some reward, or avoid some punishment.
- In **psychology**, it is sometimes called self-regulation.

Galatians 5:23, "[Self-Control is a Fruit of the Spirit.]
"…Meekness, temperance: against such there is no law."

- ➤ Father God, give me the grace, your divine enablement to exercise self-control in every area of my life, in Jesus' name.

43

Day 14

Key Verses: 3 John 1-2 & Isaiah 58:6-9

3 John 1-2 (KJV),*"1 The elder unto the wellbeloved Gaius, whom I love in the truth. 2 Beloved, I wish above all things that thou mayest **prosper** and be in health, even as thy soul **prospereth."**

> **Isaiah 58:6-8** (KJV), **"6** *Is not this the fast that I have chosen? to loose the bands of wickedness, to undo the heavy burdens, and to let the oppressed go free, and that ye break every yoke? 7 Is it not to deal thy bread to the hungry, and that thou bring the poor that are cast out to thy house? when thou seest the naked, that thou cover him; and that thou hide not thyself from thine own flesh? 8 Then shall thy light break forth as the morning, and **thine health shall spring forth speedily**: and thy righteousness shall go before thee; the glory of the Lord shall be thy reward."*

Prayer Point: Cause me to prosper in health & break me out of every addiction I have (physically, emotionally, mentally, and spiritually)

Definition:
Prosper

- To be fortunate or successful, especially in terms of one's finances.
- To thrive, to succeed, in a healthy way.

> *Joshua 1:8, "This book of the law shall not depart out of thy mouth; but thou shalt meditate therein day and night, that thou*

44

*mayest observe to do according to all that is written therein: for then thou shalt make thy way **prosper**ous, and then thou shalt have good success."*

Deuteronomy 29:9, *"Keep therefore the words of this covenant, and do them, that ye may prosper in all that ye do."*

Psalm 1:3, *"And he shall be like a tree planted by the rivers of water, that bringeth forth his fruit in his season; his leaf also shall not wither; and whatsoever he doeth shall prosper."*

Psalm 35:27, *"Let them shout for joy, and be glad, that favour my righteous cause: yea, let them say continually, Let the Lord be magnified, which hath pleasure in the **prosper**ity of his servant."*

> ➤ Father God, give the grace to obey Your Word and adhere to Your commandments, so that I may prosper and succeed in body, soul, spirit and every area of my life, in Jesus' name.

Day 15

Key Verses: Matthew 28:18- 20 (KJV)

Matthew 28:18-20, *"18 And Jesus came and spake unto them, saying, All power is given unto me in heaven and in earth. 19 Go ye therefore, and teach all nations, baptizing them in the name of the Father, and of the Son, and of the Holy Ghost: 20 Teaching them to observe all things whatsoever I have commanded you: and, lo, I am with you always, even unto the end of the world. Amen."*

Prayer Point: Use me to lead someone to Christ, in Jesus' name.

Day 16

Key Verses: Malachi 3:10-12

Malachi 3:10-12 (KJV), *"10 Bring ye all the tithes into the storehouse, that there may be meat in mine house, and prove me now herewith, saith the Lord of hosts, if I will not open you the windows of heaven, and pour you out a blessing, that there shall not be room enough to receive it. 11 And I will rebuke the devourer for your sakes, and he shall not destroy the fruits of your ground; neither shall your vine cast her fruit before the time in the field, saith the Lord of hosts. 12 And all nations shall call you blessed: for ye shall be a delightsome land, saith the Lord of hosts."*

Prayer Point: Give me grace and enable me to tithe consistently, in Jesus' name.

Day 17

Key Verses: James 5:13-16

Prayer Point: Heal those who are sick, afflicted or injured.

> **James 5:13-16** (KJV), *"13 Is any among you afflicted? let him pray. Is any merry? let him sing psalms. 14 Is any sick among you? let him call for the elders of the church; and let them pray over him, anointing him with oil in the name of the Lord: 15 And the prayer of faith shall save the sick, and the Lord shall raise him up; and if he have committed sins, they shall be forgiven him. 16 Confess your faults one to another, and pray one for another, that ye may be healed. The effectual fervent prayer of a righteous man availeth much."*

Definitions:
Sickness

- The condition of being sick, illness, a disease, a malady.
- A defective or unsound condition in one's body.

Affliction

- a condition of pain, suffering and distress.

Exodus 23:25, *"And ye shall serve the Lord your God, and he shall bless thy bread, and thy water; and I will take **sickness** away from the midst of thee."*

2 Chronicles 32:24, *"In those days Hezekiah was sick to the death, and prayed unto the Lord: and he spake unto him, and he gave him a sign."*

Matthew 8:16, *"When the even was come, they brought unto him many that were possessed with devils: and he cast out the spirits with his word, and healed all that were sick:"*

Mark 1:34, *"And he healed many that were **sick** of divers diseases, and cast out many devils; and suffered not the devils to speak, because they knew him."*

John 11:4, *"When Jesus heard that, he said, This **sickness** is not unto death, but for the glory of God, that the Son of God might be glorified thereby."*

> ➤ Father God, heal me from all manner of sickness and disease, in Jesus' name.

Exodus 3:7, *"And the Lord said, I have surely seen the affliction of my people which are in Egypt, and have heard their cry by reason of their taskmasters; for I know their sorrows;"*

Exodus 3:17, *"And I have said, I will bring you up out of the affliction of Egypt unto the land of the Canaanites, and the Hittites, and the Amorites, and the Perizzites, and the Hivites, and the Jebusites, unto a land flowing with milk and honey."*

Psalm 25:18, *"Look upon mine affliction and my pain; and forgive all my sins."*

Psalm 34:19, *"Many are the afflictions of the righteous: but the Lord delivereth him out of them all."*

> ➤ Father look upon mine **affliction** and my pain,
> forgive all my sins and heal me, in Jesus' name.

Day 18

Key Verses: Psalm 121

Prayer Point: Teach me to come to you for every void and emptiness I have which no human being can fill.

Psalm 121, *"I will lift up mine eyes unto the hills, from whence cometh my help. 2 My help cometh from the Lord, which made heaven and earth. 3 He will not suffer thy foot to be moved: He that keepeth thee will not slumber. 4 Behold, He that keepeth Israel shall neither slumber nor sleep. 5 The Lord is thy keeper: the Lord is thy shade upon thy right hand. 6 The sun shall not smite thee by day nor the moon by night. 7 The Lord shall preserve thee from all evil: He shall preserve thy soul. 8 The Lord shall preserve thy going out and thy coming in from this time forth, and even for evermore.*

> ➤ Father God, let it be so for me, in Jesus' name.

Day 19

Key Verses: Matthew 25:31-36

Prayer Point: Teach me to share what I have with others who are less fortunate.

Matthew 25:31-45, *"31 When the Son of man shall come in his glory, and all the holy angels with him, then shall he sit upon the throne of his glory: 32 And before him shall be gathered all nations: and he shall separate them one from another, as a shepherd divideth his sheep from the goats: 33 And he shall set the sheep on his right hand, but the goats on the left. 34 Then shall the King say unto them on his right hand, Come, ye blessed of my Father, inherit the kingdom prepared for you from the foundation of the world: 35 For I was an hungered, and ye gave me meat: I was thirsty, and ye gave me drink: I was a stranger, and ye took me in: 36 Naked, and ye clothed me: I was sick, and ye visited me: I was in prison, and ye came unto me. 37 Then shall the righteous answer him, saying, Lord, when saw we thee an hungered, and fed thee? or thirsty, and gave thee drink? 38 When saw we thee a stranger, and took thee in? or naked, and clothed thee? 39 Or when saw we thee sick, or in prison, and came unto thee? 40 And the King shall answer and say unto them, Verily I say unto you, Inasmuch as ye have done it unto one of the least of these my brethren, ye have done it unto me. 41 Then shall he say also unto them on the left hand, Depart from me, ye cursed, into everlasting fire, prepared for the devil and his angels:*

42 For I was an hungered, and ye gave me no meat: I was thirsty, and ye gave me no drink: 43 I was a stranger, and ye took me not in: naked, and ye clothed me not: sick, and in prison, and ye visited me not. 44 Then shall they also answer him, saying, Lord, when saw we thee an hungered, or a thirst, or a stranger, or naked, or sick, or in prison, and did not minister unto thee? 45 Then shall he answer them, saying, verily I say unto you, Inasmuch as ye did it not to one of the least of these, ye did it not to me."

➤ Father God, teach me to share what I have with others who are less fortunate, in Jesus' name.

Day 20

Key Verse: Psalm 119:105

Psalm 119:105 (KJV), *"105 Thy word is a lamp unto my feet, and a light unto my path."*

Prayer Point: Remind me to trust your Word; not what I see.

2 Samuel 22:3, *"The God of my rock; in him will I trust: he is my shield, and the horn of my salvation, my high tower, and my refuge, my savior; thou savest me from violence."*

2 Samuel 22:31, *"As for God, his way is perfect; the word of the Lord is tried: he is a buckler to all them that trust in him."*

Psalm 5:11, *"But let all those that put their **trust** in thee rejoice: let them ever shout for joy, because thou defendest them: let them also that love thy name be joyful in thee."*

Psalm 20:7, *"Some **trust** in chariots, and some in horses: but we will remember the name of the Lord our God."*

Psalm 21:7, *"For the king **trust**eth in the Lord, and through the mercy of the most High he shall not be moved."*

Psalm 22:4. *"Our fathers **trust**ed in thee: they **trust**ed, and thou didst deliver them."*

Proverbs 3:5-6 , *"5 Trust in the Lord with all thine heart; and lean not unto thine own understanding 6 In all thy ways acknowledge him, and he shall direct thy paths."*

Father God, teach me to trust in you and direct all my paths, in Jesus' name.

Day 21

Key Verse: Philippians 1:6

Philippians 1:6 (KJV), *"⁶ Being confident of this very thing, that he which hath begun a good work in you will perform it until the day of Jesus Christ."*

Prayer Point: Remind me that everything YOU have started in me, and with me, YOU will complete.

- ➢ Father God, I thank you that You are Alpha and Omega, You are the beginning and the end, You are the First and the Last.

- ➢ I thank You that You are the Author and the Finisher, The Originator and Completer of my FAITH.

- ➢ I am confident, persuaded and convinced beyond compromise, that You will complete what You have started in me, in Jesus' name.

Amen and Amen!

Made in the USA
Las Vegas, NV
05 February 2023